Sleepy
Jesus

Pennie Kidd
Illustrations by Susie Poole

A LION BOOK

It was Christmas Eve.

God was very busy.

He mixed the colours for the

sunset and shaded the sun.

He drew the cloud curtains

together and pulled down the

heavy night sky.

God put the twinkle in the stars, pushed up the moon and sprinkled frost everywhere.

He had to work quickly.

There was no time to lose.

Tonight was very special.
Baby Jesus would be born in a
stable in Bethlehem, for there
was no room at the inn.

Mary and Joseph were staying in the stable in Bethlehem. They had come a long way. They were tired and needed to rest.

Soon Baby Jesus was born on the hay. He was very small. Mary wrapped him in a cloth and sang to him. He slept quietly and Mary called him 'Sleepy Jesus'.

While Jesus slept the birds hushed their cooing. The dogs stopped barking. The donkey stopped braying. Even the cats stopped miaowing for sleepy Jesus. Only the mice whispered in the hay.

God hung a big, bright star in the east. He hushed the blowy wind. Everything was very still and quiet.

Wise men saw the star and travelled from far away. They had presents for Baby Jesus. They knew Jesus was special.

It wasn't quiet everywhere.
High in the sky near Bethlehem
choirs of angels sang with joy
about Baby Jesus.

Shepherds heard the angels singing in the sky. The angels told them to go to see Baby Jesus.

God pushed away the heavy night sky, dimmed the twinkling stars and opened the cloud curtains. He mixed the colours for the dawn, poured the paints across the sky and made the sun shine.

Jesus stirred. He rubbed his sleepy eyes; then he opened them. He smiled. God's love shone out from Baby Jesus. God smiled. It had been a busy night!